CHILDREN'S ENCYCLOPEDIA

THE WORLD OF KNOWLEDGE

TRANSPORTATION

Manasvi Vohra

V&S PUBLISHERS

Published by:

V&S PUBLISHERS

F-2/16, Ansari road, Daryaganj, New Delhi-110002
☎ 23240026, 23240027 • *Fax:* 011-23240028
Email: info@vspublishers.com • *Website:* www.vspublishers.com

Regional Office : Hyderabad
5-1-707/1, Brij Bhawan (Beside Central Bank of India Lane)
Bank Street, Koti, Hyderabad - 500 095
☎ 040-24737290
E-mail: vspublishershyd@gmail.com

Branch Office : Mumbai
Jaywant Industrial Estate, 2nd Floor-222, Tardeo Road
Opposite Sobo Central, Mumbai - 400 034
☎ 022-23510736
E-mail: vspublishersmum@gmail.com

Follow us on:

All books available at **www.vspublishers.com**

Printed at : Repro Knowledgecast Limited, Thane

PUBLISHER'S NOTE

V&S Publishers is glad to announce the launch of a unique, set of 12 books under the head, *Children's Encyclopedia – The World of Knowledge.* The set of 12 books namely – *Physices, Chemistry, Space Science, General Sceince, Life Science, Human Body, Electronics & Communications, Scientists, Inventions & Discoveries, Transportation, The Earth, and GK (General Knowledge)* has been especially developed keeping in mind the students and children of all age groups, particularly from 6 to 14 years of age. Our main aim is to arouse the interest and solve the queries of the school children regarding the various and diverse topics of Science and help them master the subject thoroughly.

In the book, *Transportation,* focusses mainly on the *Ancient, Medieval and Modern Means of Transportation, Types of Transportation, The Roadways, The Railways, The Airways and The Waterways, Supersonic Means of Transportation, Transportation in Armed Forces* and so on...

Each chapter is followed by a section called **Quick Facts** that contains a set of interesting and fascinating facts about the topics already discussed in the chapter. At the end of the book a **Glossary** of difficult words and scientific terms to make the book complete and comprehensive is given.

Quick Facts

- We can see about 2,000 stars in the sky on a clear, dark night.

Though our aim is to be flawless, but errors might have crept in inadvertently. So we request our esteemed readers to read the book thoroughly and offer valuable suggestions wherever necessary to improve and enhance the quality of the book. Hope it interests you all and serves its purpose well.

CONTENTS

Transportation

TRANSPORTATION

Chapter - 1

INTRODUCTION TO TRANSPORTATION

What is Transportation?

Movement of people, animals and things from one place to another is called *Transportation*.

The word, 'Transportation' is made up of two Latin words, *Trans* (meaning across) and *Port* (meaning to carry). So, transportation means carrying across people or things.

Dictionary meaning: *The action of transporting someone or something or the process of being transported is called Transportation.*

Vehicles used for this movement are called **Transport**.

There are *different types of Transport for different modes of*

Transportation. For example:

- Cars, buses, trucks, cycles and bikes run on roads.
- Boats, ferries, ships and cruises move on water.
- Aeroplanes, helicopters and jets fly in air.
- Passenger trains and carrier trains run on railway tracks.

These vehicles run on fuels like *petrol, diesel and CNG*.
Some vehicles also run on *electricity*, such as the modern metro trains of today and the superfast electric trains like Rajdhani, Shatabdi, Mail trains and Express trains running across the country from one place to another.

What is 'Fuel'?

Fuel is the substance which gives energy to a vehicle for running or moving from one place to another, in the same way as you give food to your body for working and living. Thus, petrol, *diesel, CNG and electricity* are in a way the food for a vehicle.

Small and light vehicles like cars, bikes and small motorboats need less fuel and generally, run on petrol. Nowadays, with the advent of *CNG or Compressed Natural Gas*, many large and heavy vehicles like trucks, buses, tempos, ferries, which need more fuel, run on diesel or CNG. However, there are also some small vehicles, such as autorickshaws that run on CNG which are a popular means of local public transport in cities and towns.

Bigger vehicles like *aeroplanes and ships* run on large amount of fuel. Some vehicles like *trains, metro and trams* run on electricity. There are a few trains which run on steam produced by burning coal. Vehicles like *cycles* and *cycle rickshaws* do not need any fuel to run; they run by *manual pedalling*.

Quick Facts

- There are more than 600 million cars in the world.
- In Delhi, public transport like buses and autorickshaws run on CNG.
- There are about 1,080,000 CNG vehicles in India.
- The first bus was set in motion in 1662, at the initiative of Blaise Pascal. The bus was then given a travel schedule, a fixed route, a charge carrier and of course, horses to put it in motion.
- In 1775, James Watt perfected the steam engine setting in motion a new era of public transportation. From then onwards, trains, buses, boats, etc., all began using the steam engine to "improve" the life of the masses.
- In 1807, was invented the first steam vessel that carries passengers, even today in several parts of the world.
- In 1825, was built the world's first public railway between the cities of Stockton and Darlington.
- The first subway in the world was built in London in 1863.

Chapter - 2

ANCIENT TRANSPORTATION

The term, 'ancient transportation' means the various means of transport used in the early age or ancient period.

During the early age, man used to walk to travel from one place to another or use animals like horses, camels, elephants, etc for transportation. This used to take a long time for one group of people to move from one settlement to another. After sometime, the early man started using stone and wood to make tools. With the use of these tools, he started making vehicles like carts and boats.

For crossing a water body like a lake or a river, he used to swim and travel. After sometime, the early man began using wood logs tied together by ropes to make rafts. In a few years, he also started making small boats from wood, for fishing and travelling.

Dugout Canoe

A dugout canoe is a boat which is made out of a tree trunk. It was first invented in the Stone Age by the early man. He used whole logs of tree trunks to make a dugout canoe with the help of fire and stone tools.

Dugout canoes were used mainly for carrying things, fishing and for carrying troops.

Invention of Wheel

After the early man invented wheel, vehicles like carts pulled by animals were used for transportation. Animals like horse, ox, bullocks and camels were used to pull these carts. This was the best means of transportation as man could carry lots of things on carts and travel easily from one place to another.

Quick Facts

- Man used wood and ropes to make animal carts. Later, he also put up a roof on the cart to shelter from rains, winds and heat.
- We can still find similar bullock carts in many small villages of our country.
- The first dugout canoe was invented in the Stone Age.
- The first wheeled cart was invented in 3500 BC.
- Horses were domesticated for transportation around 2000 BC.

Chapter - 3

MEDIEVAL TRANSPORTATION

The medieval means of transportation was used in the medieval age and it varied from region to region.

Roads and Bridges

Roads came into existence with the advent of the medieval age. These roads were paved with stones and bricks. The development of paved roads made transportation easier for people.

Still, paved roads were not common everywhere. These were present only in the significant areas like city centres or shopping malls, trading areas, royal and government residences, etc.

The Roman road networks made during the Roman Empire are still famous.

In Europe, rivers were made crossable with the advent of bridges. These bridges were made up of stones and bricks and could bear light to medium load.

Transportation

Horses – Horses were the main animals to be used for transportation. Rich people travelled by horses. Goods were transported by 'pack horses', i.e., horses with bags of goods on both their sides.

Wagons – Wagons were improved version of the wooden carts. They were used mainly to carry goods.

The Two-Mule Litter

Litters – Litters were wooden boxes big enough for a person to sit, supported by two parallel poles at two sides of the box. These poles were attached to two horses, one at front and one at back. These horses were specially trained to walk at the same pace.

Did You Know?

The first *President of India, Dr. Rajendra Prasad,* arrived in the *first Republic Day parade in a horse carriage.*

Chariots – Chariots were improved version of horse carriages. They were mostly used by army troops during a battle.

Coach – A coach is considered to be the first public transport. It was a covered carriage with a door and a window, in which four people could sit at the same time. It was attached to a horse and was driven by a coachman.

Mast ships – Ships were improved by erecting a cloth mast against a pole in it. Mast ships had better speed which made transportation easier and speedier.

Quick Facts

- A litter is very similar to a palanquin used in India to carry new brides. The only difference is that palanquins were carried by men on their shoulders.

- Carriages were horse driven wooden vehicles.

- The advent of the British saw trams being introduced in many cities including Mumbai and Kolkata. They are still in use in Kolkata and provide an emission-free means of transport.

Chapter - 4

TRANSPORTATION IN MODERN AGE

Modern Age transportation consists of vehicles like cars, buses, bikes, aeroplanes, trains, motorboats, etc.

Invention of Automobile

An automobile is a four-wheeled vehicle with a motor to run it. A car is a best example of an automobile. The word, *automobile* is derived from a mix of Greek word, *autos* which means 'self' and Latin word, *mobilis* which means 'movable'. Thus, automobile means a vehicle which can run on its own.

Following the development of an automobile, many other vehicles using similar technology have been brought on roads. Buses, trucks, bikes – all of them use their respective engines to run.

Did You Know?

The term, *Car* is derived from the Latin word, *Carrus* or *Carrum* which means 'wheeled vehicle'.

INVENTION OF AIRCRAFT

An Aircraft

The Modern Age saw some of the greatest inventions in the field of air transportation. Prior to the modern age, there were some attempts to make humans fly in the air. These efforts resulted into – kites, hot-air balloons and gliders. But none of these attempts could be turned into successful means of transportation.

In the year, **1903, Wright brothers**, **Orville** and **Wilbur** demonstrated the first *ever airplane with a propeller*.

Some Types of Aircraft

These were run on not so powerful engines and were not used much for commercial purposes.

Subsonic – Boeing 747 is an example of *subsonic passenger and cargo plane*. It flies at 350-750 mph, just below the speed of sound, and is the most successful commercial aircraft.

Supersonic – A Concorde is a good example of a supersonic plane which can fly at a speed of 750-3500 mph, i.e. five times the speed of sound.

Hypersonic – A Space Shuttle is an example of hypersonic plane. A hypersonic plane is attached to a rocket which flies 5-10 times more than the speed of sound, i.e., 3500-7000 mph.

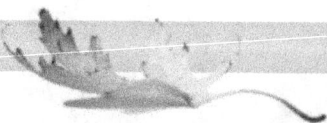

Modern Railways

The modern system of railways was born in England in 1820s. Steam locomotives were the first modernised development or offering to the world. By 1900s, diesel engine locomotives came into use. By 1970, most of the railway networks in the world had started *diesel engine locomotives*.

Did You Know?

The first steam engine was invented by **Thomas Newcomen**.

Quick Facts

- With the invention of wheels came the cycle which is still a very popular form of transport. In fact, in China it is the only form of conveyance for the common man. It does not require any fuel and therefore, does not harm the environment. It is an eco-friendly vehicle.

- The first invention that made transport truly fast was the invention of the steam engine. This led to the railways.

- The petrol engine soon changed the whole scene by making the motorcar possible. Today, of course, we have motorcycles, motorcars and diesel run trucks.

- The first reliable motor vehicle to be used as a public transport was the electric train.

- The bulkiest of materials can easily be transported from one end of the country to the other end by means of trucks or by railways.

- Pipeline transport sends goods through a pipe, most commonly liquid and gases are sent, but pneumatic tubes can also send solid capsules using compressed air. For liquids/gases, any chemically stable liquid or gas can be sent through a pipeline. Short-distance systems exist for sewage, slurry, water and beer, while long-distance networks are used for petroleum and natural gas.

- Cable transport is a broad mode where vehicles are pulled by cables instead of an internal power source.

- Spaceflight is the transport out of the Earth's atmosphere into outer space by means of a spacecraft.

- The first modern rapid transit in India was the Kolkata Metro, with operations starting in 1984. The Delhi Metro in the capital city of New Delhi and is the second conventional metro which began operations in 2002.The Namma Metro in Bengaluru is India's third operational rapid transit beginning operations in 2011. Currently, rapid transit systems have been deployed in these cities and more are under construction or in planning in several major cities of India.

- The Metro Systems under construction are the Mumbai Metro, the Rapid Metro Rail Gurgaon, the Jaipur Metro, the Chennai Metro, the Navi Mumbai Metro, the Hyderabad Metro, the Kochi Metro, etc.

Chapter - 5

METHODS OF TRANSPORTATION

Transportation can be classified into three different categories depending upon the methods. The three methods of transportation are:

1. Manual
2. Animal Powered
3. Mechanical

Manual

Manual or human-powered transport is that type of transport where a man uses his muscle-power and energy to move the vehicle. These vehicles don't need any machine or scientific technology to run. Most of the vehicles used in the ancient times till the start of the modern age were manual/human-powered. Some of the examples of manual means of transport are:

- Hand carts
- Bicycles

- Small boats
- Canoes
- Rafts

Advantages of Manual Transport

- Low cost – These means of transport save money on fuel as well as on the maintenance.

- Save environment – These help in saving our environment because they don't run on pollution emitting fuels.

Animal Powered

Animal powered transport is that type of transport where animals are used to move the vehicles. Like manual means of transport, these vehicles also do not need any fuel or machine to run. These run by the muscle strength of animals like horses, camels, oxen, etc.

Depending upon the region and the climate, different animals are used to power the vehicles. For example, in plains, animals like horses and oxen are used to pull the vehicles. In hilly terrains, mules and ponies are used while in snowy region, animals like yaks and big dogs are used for this purpose. Some examples of animal-powered transport are:

- Bullock cart
- Horse carriage
- Sleigh
- Sledge

Animal powered transportation has same advantages as that of human powered, i.e., it saves cost as well as *environment pollution*. Moreover, it is better than human powered transport as animals have better strength and capacity than humans.

Mechanical

Mechanical transport is that type of transport which uses motors and machines to run. Unlike manual and animal-powered vehicles, these vehicles require fuel to generate energy for them to work. Today, most of the world uses mechanical transportation. Some examples are:

- Cars
- Buses
- Trains
- Aeroplanes

Advantages of Mechanical Transportation:

High speed – These vehicles are very fast as compared to manual and animal-powered transportation as they are made using an advanced technology.

- **Saves time –** These means of transport save time during transportation because of their high speed.

- **Convenient –** They are very comfortable and convenient to use. For example: Most of them, nowadays, have air conditioners, comfortable seats, music systems, etc.

Quick Facts

- Pollution emitting fuels are those which generate smoke after being used. Fuels like petrol, diesel and coal emit smoke which cause pollution in the atmosphere. We must make sure to use these fuels in small quantities to help keep our environment pollution free.

- Other environmental impacts of transport systems include traffic congestion and automobile-oriented urban sprawl, which can consume natural habitats and agricultural lands. By reducing transportation emissions globally, it is predicted that there will be significant positive effects on the Earth's air quality, acid rain, smog and climate change.

- The Rail based transit systems in India include the Suburban Railway (also referred as EMU/DMU), Rail Rapid Transit or Metro Systems and Monorail.

- The present suburban railway services in India are limited and are operational only in Mumbai, Kolkata, Chennai, Delhi and MMTS Hyderabad.

- The first modern rapid transit in India was the Kolkata Metro, with operations starting in 1984. The Delhi Metro in the capital city of New Delhi is the second conventional metro which began operations in 2002.

- The Namma Metro in Bengaluru is India's third operational rapid transit beginning operations in 2011.

TYPES OF TRANSPORTATION

Depending upon the passenger usage, transportation is divided into two categories:

- Public
- Private

Public Transportation

Public transportation is that which is managed by government/ administrative authorities. Public transport, usually, runs on a fixed time and on a fixed route. For example, buses, trains, metros, taxis, autorickshaws, etc are all means of public transport.

In India, public transport, such as buses and autorickshaws come under the state control, whereas, taxis are owned by private companies. **The Indian Railways** is the biggest mode of public transport and is controlled by the Ministry of Railways under the Government of India.

Did You Know?

Around 30 million people travel in the Indian Railways, daily.

Public transportation is also a good source of revenue generation for the government.

Advantages of Using Public Transport

- Low cost
- Reduces pollution
- Reduces traffic jams
- Reduces usage of fuel
- Best means of transportation for people without private vehicles

Private Transportation

The Private means of Transport are those which are owned by individuals for their private use. For example, cars, bikes, cycles, private buses, vans, helicopters, etc. These are not available for the general public. People use private vehicles to meet their personal demands.

In India, out of the total registered vehicles per year, 95% are privately owned.

Did You Know?

In Delhi, an average of *965 private vehicles* are registered daily.

Today, many privately owned cars are running on CNG and LPG like most of the public transport, in India. This helps in keeping a check on pollution and reducing individual carbon footprint.

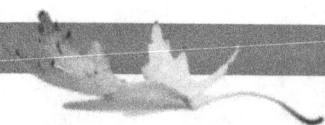

Advantages of Using Private Transport

- ❦ It offers flexibility.
- ❦ It is not time bound and scheduled.
- ❦ It saves time unlike public transport.
- ❦ It provides privacy to the users.

Means of Transportation

'Means of transport' is a term which describes and distinguishes different ways of transportation. There are *four different means of transportation - Roadways, Railways, Waterways and Airways.* For Roadways, the examples are cars, buses, vans, jeeps, trucks, etc. For Railways, the examples are Express trains, Mail trains, Metros, and for Waterways, we have ships, steamers, motorboats, cruises, boats, etc. For Airways, we have aeroplanes, jet planes, helicopters, etc.

Quick Facts

- Among all the metro cities of India, Delhi has the maximum number of vehicles (about 4.8 million) on road, followed by Bangalore or Bengaluru (around 3.1 million) and Chennai (about 3 million).

- India has one of the largest road networks in the world, aggregating to about 33 lakh kilometres at present. The country's road network consists of National Highways, State Highways, Expressways, major/other district roads and in villages—the rural roads.

- Approximately, 90 percent of the country's trade by volume (70 percent in terms of value) is moved by sea. India has the largest merchant shipping fleet among the developing countries.

- The coastline of India is dotted with 12 Major Ports and about 200 Non-major Ports. The Major Ports are under the purview of the central government, while the Non-major Ports come under the jurisdiction of the respective state governments.

- India has about 14,500 km of navigable inland waterways which comprise rivers, canals, backwaters, creeks, etc.

- The Indian Railways is the largest railway system in the world under a single management.

- The Airports Authority of India (AAI) was created on 1st April 1995 by combining the International Airports Authority of India and the National Airports Authority.

- There are a total of about 20 international airports and many domestic airports.

Chapter - 7

THE ROADWAYS

A road is a route of travel which connects cities, towns and villages with each other. In a vast country like India, roads play a very important role in connecting the interior rural areas to urban regions.

Stone-paved Roads

The stone-paved roads were first built in Mesopotamia and the Indus Valley Civilization.

Construction of Roads

Modern roads are made up of materials like concrete, asphalt, stone and gravel. First of all, the process starts with removing obstacles in the route by blasting of huge rocks, digging of the earth, removal of stones and cutting trees. After the track is cleared, it is then paved with a mixture of asphalt, concrete, stone and gravel.

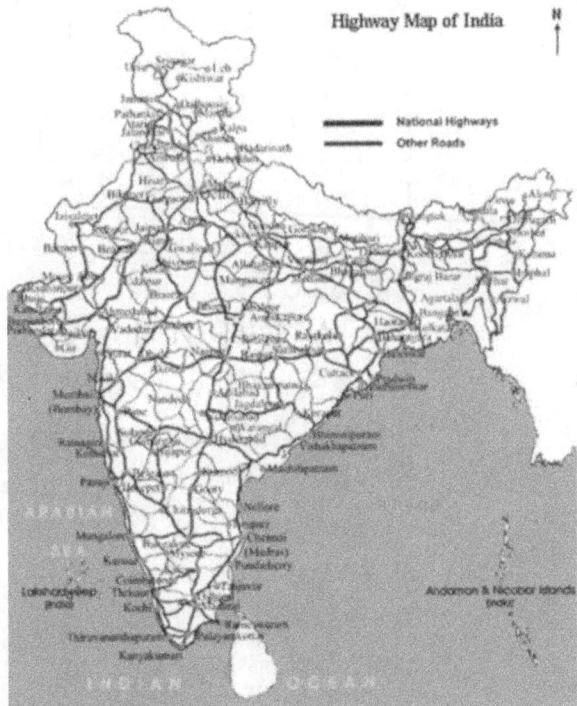

Highway Map of India

National Highways
Other Roads

Did You Know?

India has the third largest road network in the world with approximately 3,383,344 kilometres of roads.

Types of Roads

The roads are classified into:

- **National Highways** – These are the roads connecting the state capitals and are financed by the central government.

- **Expressways** – There are about 11 Super Expressways in India. They are the Ahmedabad Vadodara Expressway, the Mumbai-Pune Expressway, the Jaipur-Kishangarh Expressway, the Allahabad Bypass, the Ambala Chandigarh Expressway, the Chennai Bypass, the Delhi-Gurgaon Expressway, the Delhi-Noida Direct Flyway,

the Hyderabad Elevated Expressway and the Hosur Road Elevated Expressway. There are many more expressways in India which are under construction, or are already approved, but work has not started yet.

- **State Highways** – These are the roads connecting important cities in a state and are financed by the state government.

- **District Highways** – These are the roads connecting district headquarters and important towns in the district with state and national highways. They are funded by the Zila Parishads.

- **Village Roads** – These are the roads connecting several villages and to the nearest district highway. These are the financed by the Village Panchayats.

Transportation

Vehicles running on roads constitute the roadways transportation. These are generally driven by automobiles with the use of motors.

Vehicles used for transportation purpose on roads are divided into:

- Passenger carrier vehicles
- Freight carrier vehicles

Passenger Carrier Vehicles

Vehicles which are used to transport people are called passenger carriers. For example:

- Cycles
- Bikes
- Cars
- Autorickshaws
- Buses

People mostly drive cars, bikes and cycles for their private use. There are more than 51922 thousand two-wheelers and around 9451 thousand four-wheelers (as recorded in the year, 2004) running on roads in India.

Vehicles like buses and auto rickshaws are generally used for public transit. In India, public transport is the most widely used transport system.

The term, 'Public Transit' is used to describe the transportation facility provided by the government to the people.

An automobile is a passenger vehicle run with the help of a motor.

Freight Carrier Vehicles

Vehicles which are used to carry goods are called *freight carriers*. For example:

- Trucks
- Tempos
- Lorries
- Trailers

These vehicles save time and energy while transporting goods.

Quick Facts

- In the year, 1897, the first car ran on the Indian roads.
- As long as 2600 km in length, the Grand Trunk Road (G.T. Road) is the busiest road in India.
- The Indian roads are left-hand-drive.
- Cars are right-hand-drive.
- Wearing seat belts is obligatory.
- Distances are mentioned in kilometres.
- Stretches of both main and country roads are punctuated with petrol (gas) stations. Still, there is a considerable distance between them.

Chapter - 8

THE RAILWAYS

The Railways constitute of a pair of parallel metal rail tracks fixed to sleepers, on which trains run carrying people and goods.

Unlike roadways, where vehicles run on prepared surfaces (roads), rail vehicles are guided to their way by the rail tracks. But, like roadways, the railways are also an important means of transportation.

The Beginning of the Railways

The first train in India ran from Bombay (now Mumbai) to Thane in the year, 1853. The first locomotive was the **steam engine**, which used **coals** to create steam.

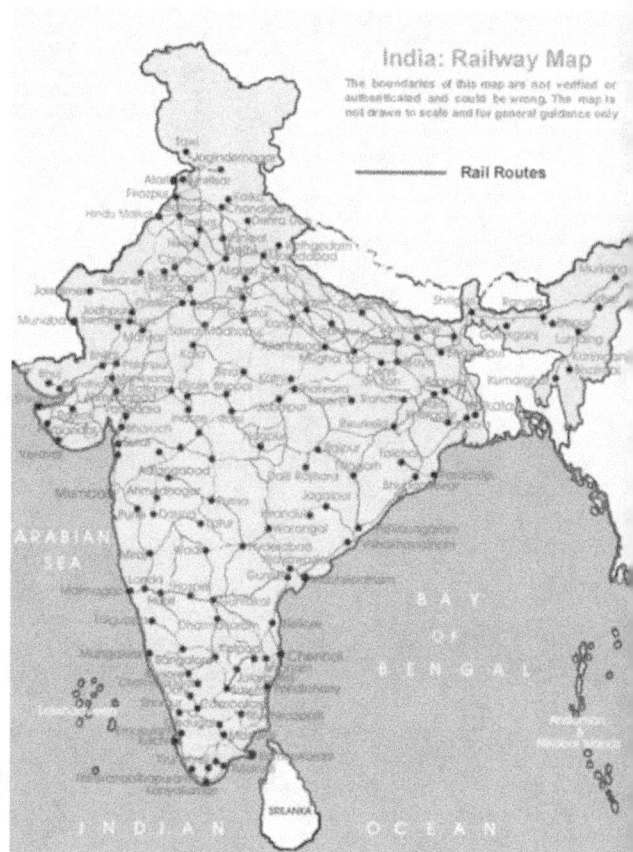

Types of Rails

- **Broad gauge** – This is the most widely used railway track in India as most of the traffic is on the broad gauge.

- **Metre gauge** – This is used in the regions with less traffic.

- **Narrow gauge** – This is mostly used in the hilly terrain of the country.

Types of Trains

- **Passenger trains** – Trains which carry people are called passenger trains.

- **Goods trains** – Trains which carry goods, machines, vehicles, etc., from one place to another are called goods trains.

Did You Know?

In India, trains carry more than *30 million people daily* and about *2.8 million tons of load daily* from one place to another.

The Indian Railways

The Indian Railways rank **first** in *Asia* and **fourth** in the *world*. Today, more than *11000 trains* run in the railway network of our country. The length of the Indian Railways is more than **111,599 km**.

The Indian Railways is divided into the following zones:

1. Central Railways
2. Northern Railways
3. North-eastern Railways
4. North-western Railways
5. North-central Railways

6. North-east Frontier Railways

7. Eastern Railways

8. East-central Railways

9. East coast Railways

10. Western Railways

11. West-central Railways

12. Southern Railways

13. South-central Railways

14. South-western Railways

15. South-east central Railways

16. South-eastern Railways

Some of the significant rail routes which connect important cities of India are:

1. Delhi to Mumbai

2. Delhi to Kalka

3. Delhi to Chennai

4. Delhi to Aurangabad

5. Mumbai to Amritsar

6. Mumbai to Bangalore or Bengaluru

7. Mumbai to Vijayawada

8. Saharanpur to Varanasi

9. Lucknow to Guwahati

10. Kolkata to Chennai

11. Chennai to Jammu

12. Delhi to Kolkata

- The word, 'railway' was first coined in the year, 1776.

- The first railway was opened in 1825. It was the Stockton & Darlington Railroad, which was opened on September 27, 1825.

- The Indian Railways is the lifeline of the average Indians. The Indian Railways have continued to exist since more than 150 years.

- The Indian Railways employ more than 1.6 million people, thus becoming the largest utility employer in the world.

- There are more than 7,500 railway stations in India.

- There is a fleet of about 7800 locomotives in India and around 40,000 coaches.

- The establishment of the National Rail Museum took place in 1977.

- In 1986, the first Computerised Reservation System began in New Delhi.

- Sri Venkatanarasimharajuvariapeta in Tamil Nadu is the longest station name of India.

- The first electric train came into force on February 3, 1925 between Bombay VT (Mumbai) and Kurla.

Chapter - 9

THE AIRWAYS

The Airways are the fastest means of transportation in the world today. It consists of winged crafts like aeroplanes, helicopters, etc. Also, this means of transportation requires an *airbase* and a *runway* from where the planes take off as well as land on. And because of the huge size of the aircraft and the airbase, it becomes the costliest means of transportation.

Unlike other means of transportation, the airways are not divided into passenger and goods carriers. Here, big planes like *Airbuses* and *Boeings* also carry freights/goods along with the passengers.

Helicopters carry a maximum of 2-3 people at once, whereas a Boeing carries around 400-500 people.

The Airways have two branches:

💣 **International Transportation** – Planes carrying passengers as well as goods from one country to another come under international transportation. Air services like the Air India, Jet Airways, British Airways, etc provide international travel to people.

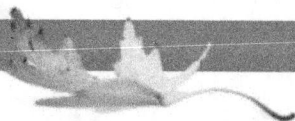

❉ **Domestic Transportation** – Planes carrying passengers as well as goods within a country, from one region to another, come under domestic transportation. Services like the Indian *Airlines, Spicejet, IndiGo*, etc are domestic airlines.

These planes are run publicly as well as privately.

The **Indian Public Sector Airways** include the **Air India** and the **Indian Airlines**. These are managed by the government and are the official airlines of India.

The Private Airlines include the **Jet Airways**, the **Kingfisher**, the **Spicejet**, etc. These are run by private companies. The private

airlines are more profit oriented, and they also provide more flexibility. They also provide private **jet planes** as well as **helicopters** to important and rich people.

Airports

Airports are the most important aspect of airway travel as these are the places, where people gather to board and de-board a plane. Airports include runways for planes to take-off as well as land.

Indira Gandhi International Airport

Some international airports of India are the *Indira Gandhi International Airport (New Delhi), Chhatrapati Shivaji Airport (Mumbai), Netaji Subhas Chandra Bose Airport (Kolkata)*, etc.

Some domestic airports of India are in cities like New Delhi, Mumbai, Lucknow, Amritsar, Chandigarh, Kolkata, Bangalore (Bengaluru), Chennai, Ahmedabad, etc.

Quick Facts

- Air India Limited is the major international carrier of the country.

- The Indian Airlines is the major domestic air carrier of the country. It operates to 57 domestic stations (including Alliance Air operations) and 17 international stations in 14 countries.

- The Pawan Hans Helicopters Limited has been providing helicopter support services to the petroleum sector including the ONGC, the Oil India Limited and the Hardy Exploration at Chennai. Apart from these, it also provides services to certain state governments and public sector undertakings and in the north-eastern states.

- The development of airports is no longer solely under the public sector; instead private participation is allowed and encouraged. An International green field airport has been developed in Cochin, Kerala, with contributions from NRIs and loans from financial institutions.

Chapter - 10

THE WATERWAYS

A waterway is an integral means of transportation in a country like ours which is a **peninsula** and where so many rivers flow across the land.

A Ship

The waterways consist of small *boats, ferries* and *steamers* moving on water bodies like *lakes* and *rivers* as well as big *watercrafts* like *ships* and *cruises* moving in seas and oceans.

Like airways, the waterways also carry passengers as well as freight together. Big watercrafts like cruises and steamers carry tonnes of freight along with a large number of passengers. Some ships are used exclusively for trading purposes and they carry only goods. Small watercrafts like boats and motorboats as well as ferries are mainly used for passenger transportation. *Canoes and rafts* are mostly used in water sports than for the purpose of transportation.

A Motor Boat

Did You Know?

A ferry is a medium sized ship which can carry people, cargo as well as small to medium sized vehicles from one shore to another.

Ports and Harbours

A port is a place where big trading ships are loaded and unloaded and people can embark and disembark the ships. *India has a coastline of about 7600 km.* Thus, there are as many as *13 major seaports* along the coastline. *Mumbai, Chennai, Kolkata,*

Paradip, Cochin and Port Blair are some of the major ports. Calicut, Porbandar and Trivandrum are some of the minor ports in India.

A harbour is a place where ships, boats and ferries take shelter.

There are two types of harbours:

- **Natural Harbour –** It is a landform with natural cavity along the shore, where a part of the river/ sea/ ocean is protected.

- **Artificial Harbour –** An artificial harbour is built by man along the busy sea shores to act as ports.

Did You Know?

Jebel Ali in Dubai is the largest artificially created harbour in the world.

Goa, Kochi, Panjim, Pondicherry and Mangalore are some of the well-known harbours in India.

Quick Facts

- A peninsula is a piece of land which is surrounded by water from three sides. India is a peninsula as it is surrounded by the Bay of Bengal in the right, the Arabian Sea in the left and the Indian Ocean from below.

- India has an extensive network of inland waterways in the form of rivers, canals, backwaters and creeks.

- Ship transport is watercraft carrying people (passengers) or goods (cargo). Sea transport has been the largest carrier of freight throughout the recorded history.

- The historical development of water-based transportation is connected to the importance of domestic and international trade in the world.

- Modern ferries, cruise ships and many types of recreational boats carry passengers for purposes ranging from daily business commuting to fishing to sightseeing. The ferry system in Halifax, Nova Scotia (Canada) demonstrates the importance of waterways for transportation.

Chapter - 11

SUPERSONIC MEANS OF TRANSPORTATION

A supersonic means of transportation is a vehicle which runs at a speed greater than that of the sound. In the whole universe, **sound** and **light** are the two fastest travelling entities. By developing a supersonic vehicle, man has mastered at least, one entity of this nature.

A Supersonic Vehicle

The speed of sound is about 343.2 metres/second or 768 miles/hour. A supersonic vehicle has a faster speed than that.

The idea of an automobile with a speed greater than that of sound started fascinating scientists and researchers in the early 1950s. Since then, scientific technology has been able to develop supersonic aircraft, such as the *Concorde* and *Tupolev Tu – 144*.

Concorde

Concorde is a supersonic aircraft used for transporting passengers. It is a product of United Kingdom.

Since their inception, a total of 20 Concordes were built by the Ministry of Civil Aviation. Out of these, around nine were purchased by state-owned airlines of Britain and France, the British Airways and the Air France.

Tupolev Tu – 144

Tupolev Tu – 144 is a Soviet supersonic aircraft. It is designed by the Soviet Tupolev Design Bureau, under the leadership of *Alexei Tupolev*.

In December 1968, Tupolev became the first supersonic plane to take flight, two months earlier than Concorde. But it was launched as a commercial air passenger after almost two years of Concorde's launch, in 1977.

Tupolev flew *55 scheduled passenger flights* and a total of about *102 commercial flights*. It was later used by the *National Aeronautics and Space Administration (NASA)* for supersonic research and by the Soviet Space programme to train spacecraft pilots.

Did You Know?

The first Tupolev was unveiled in January, 1962.

Advantages of Supersonic Transportation

- Very high speed as compared to the conventional transportation modes.

- Good efficiency, i.e., able to be more frequent, almost three times the conventional airplanes.

Disadvantages of Supersonic Transportation

- Excessive noise generations known as *sonic booms*.
- High development cost.
- Massive weight.
- High cost per passenger as compared to the conventional airplanes.

Quick Facts

- Supersonic airliners' greater speed and efficiency over their conventional counterparts have made them objects of numerous recent and ongoing design studies.

- The drawbacks and design challenges are excessive noise generation (at takeoff and due to sonic booms during flight), high development costs, expensive construction materials, great weight, and an increased cost per seat over subsonic airliners. Despite these challenges, the Concorde was operated profitably in a niche market for over 27 years.

- Supersonic vehicle speeds demand narrower wing and fuselage designs, and are subject to greater stresses and temperatures. This leads to aeroelasticity problems, which require heavier structures to minimise unwanted flexing.

Chapter - 12

TRANSPORTATION IN ARMED FORCES

Armed Forces are a very important part of a nation. *Transportation plays a significant role in the defence of a country.*

Transportation through Roadways – Roads play an important role in defence. Roadways allow tanks and artilleries to be smoothly transported to the front.

Uses:

- ❧ Ease of transportation of soldiers, tanks, missiles and weapons to the front.

- ❧ Helps in carrying rations and other requirements to the army camps.

- ❧ Tanks equipped with radars help in locating the enemy camps.

Did You Know?

Armed Forces are one of the firsts to help in the rescue operations in case of a disaster like earthquake, flood, tsunami, etc.

Transportation through Airways –
Fighter planes, jets and defence helicopters use airways to fight the enemies. Tanker aircrafts and transport aircrafts are helpful in operational activities.

Uses:

- Helps in transportation of soldiers to difficult terrains like hills and snow-capped mountains.
- Carry rations for the soldiers in these difficult terrains.
- Helps in rescue operations.
- Helps in restoration work in the event of a natural calamity.

Transportation through Waterways –
Defence services use submarines, ships, motorboats, etc for safeguarding of the country.

Uses:

- The Coast Guard uses ships to guard the coast of the country against smugglers, pirates and other enemies.
- The Navy uses watercrafts to defend and patrol the seas and oceans of its territory.

- Submarines gather information regarding the enemies for safeguarding of the nation.

Quick Facts

- A submarine is a water craft which moves below the surface of water (under the seas and oceans) and gathers information. The main purpose of a submarine is to be kept hidden all the time, while it collects important data and locates any danger.

- The Indian Air Force has many aircrafts of Russian, Israel, British, French, U.S. and Indian origin.

- The Indian Navy presently has one aircraft carrier ship in its active service.

- The MiG fighter planes of Russian origin have had the most number of accidents in the recent times.

Chapter - 13

TRANSPORTATION FOR PEOPLE WITH DISABILITIES

Unlike a few decades back, the transportation scenario for disabled people has changed considerably. Many nations across the globe have initiated transportation facilities for people with physical disabilities.

Changes in Transportation Facilities

There have been many remarkable changes in the transportation facilities initiated for the disabled people.

Private Transportation

Wheelchair – Automated wheelchairs with brakes are an advanced mode of transportation for physically disabled people. These are easy and efficient to use.

Electric Scooter – An electric scooter is the latest introduction in the domain of private transportation for physically disabled people.

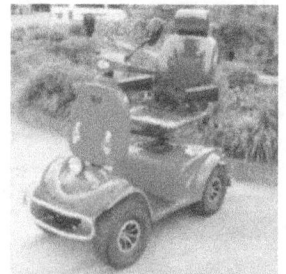

It runs on electricity, can be recharged easily, and is compact and lightweight.

Customisation of car with low floor folding platform for easy shifting from wheelchair to car seat is readily available. Moreover, cars specially designed for disabled people are hitting the market speedily.

Car hand controls are available in the market. These are alternatives for car controls like brakes, clutches and accelerators, which require footwork. These hand controls are customised for people keeping in mind their handicap.

Public Transportation

Buses – Low floor hybrid buses are being designed keeping in mind the disabled. They have low floors which align parallel to the bus stops

and footpaths so that people on wheelchair can move into the bus without difficulty and on their own. These buses have designated space for wheelchairs, along with safety belts.

Metro Trains – Metro trains in Delhi is one of the most disabled-friendly public transports in the world. It provides lifts for the disabled people to move from one platform to another. Also, because the height of the platform is same to that of the metro doors, wheelchair bound people find it easy to board the train. Moreover, the space designated for disabled people makes their commuting easy and hassle free.

Railway Trains – Some trains have special places reserved for wheelchairs in each compartment. This facility has not yet arrived in India. Apart from these, new constructions are being made keeping in mind the facilities for the disabled people. Footpaths are being provided with a slope for the usage of the disabled. Many public places like airports, malls, railway stations, etc are being equipped with ramp walks.

Quick Facts

- The Da Paratransit Programs or ADA Paratransit Systems are run by all fixed-route bus systems in Connecticut. Each agency provides transportation for residents within their service areas who are unable to use local buses. Participants must apply for the service, provide documented proof of their disability and pay a set fee for each trip that they take, according to the Connecticut State Department of Transportation (DOT).

- Senior/Disabled Ride Programs: Dial-A-Ride Programs are offered by some cities or towns and community councils in Connecticut and other parts of the United States. Transportation is provided to local destinations, such as banks, hospitals, stores, etc.

- While technology in locomotion and mobility for the disabled has taken great strides worldwide, India is also forging ahead to modernise its age-old tricycles and wheelchairs by designing user-friendly appliances and means of transport for the disabled.

Chapter - 14

TRANSPORTATION WORLDWIDE

Let's have a look at the unique modes of transportation in different parts of the world. For Example, *the Bullet Train of Japan.*

Also known as *Shinkansen*, meaning 'new trunk line', the Bullet Train is one of the most famous high-speed train networks of the world. Started in 1964, this network currently has about 2,387.7 km long line. The bullet trains touch the maximum speed of 149-80 mph. A bullet can be *400m long with 16 coaches.*

According to 2007 report, around 353.18 million passengers used the bullet trains in a year.

Aerial Tramways

Aerial tramway, ropeway or *cable car* is an aerial lift which is used for transportation mainly in the hilly regions. A cable car is a passenger cabin suspended in the air by the support of two fixed cables and propelled forward by a motor.

These cable cars are used for moving people in difficult terrains, in mining and in tourism. Recently, they have also become a part of public transport in USA – the Roosevelt Island Tramway in New York City and the Portland Aerial Tram.

Monorail

A monorail is a train which moves on a single rail line. The first mono rail ran in the year, 1820 in Russia. Today, there are mono rails operating in countries like South Africa, China, Japan, Singapore, Malaysia, Thailand, Philippines, Australia, America and many more.

The world's busiest monorail line is the Tokyo monorail which serves approximately 127,000 passengers per day. It has served over 1.5 billion passengers since 1964.

Trams

A tram is a passenger carrying vehicle which runs on rail tracks laid on roads. Trams usually run within a city unlike passenger trains. They run on electricity provided by a cable running along its path. Great Britain, France, Ireland and United States have tram networks in their public transportation. The tram network in Melbourne, Australia and the Silesian Interurbans in Poland are the largest tram networks in the world. In India, Kolkata trams are the oldest in Asia, running since 1902, but now they have almost become obsolete.

Rapid Transit

A rapid transit system is an *electric railway network* in *urban areas*. It is also known as *underground, tube, subway, or metro* in different parts of the world. The rapid transit lines are laid in the underground level of the city or on an elevated rail line in the air.

Some of the popular rapid transit networks in the world are the London Tube, the New York City Subway, the Moscow Metro, the Tokyo Subway and the Seoul Metropolitan Subway. *In India, the Kolkata Metro* was the first rapid transit network, followed by *Delhi* and *Bangalore (Bengaluru)*.

Quick Facts

- USA is followed up by Japan, while UK, Germany and France occupy the 3rd, 4th and 5th positions in the frequency of air travel in the world.

- Shipping carries most of the world's bulky goods. The desire for speedy travel has been satisfied by high-tech vessels like hydrofoils and hovercraft. Japan has around 8462 vessels followed up by Panama with 6143 vessels. USA and Russia are in the 3rd and 4th positions with 5642 and 4694 vessels respectively. China is in the 5th place.

Chapter - 15

FUTURISTIC MEANS OF TRANSPORTATION

With huge daily consumption of non-renewable sources of energy for transportation, the ecological balance is getting disturbed day by day. To restore this ecological balance, we must think of some alternative sources of fuel energy to run our means of transport.

A Jet Scooter by Norio Fujikawa of Japan is a concept vehicle that comprises both the look of a traditional scooter and at the same time, the essence of a futuristic means of transportation. As the name denotes, this vehicle comprises a jet engine and houses only one rider.

Solar Energy

Solar energy is a *never-ending source of energy*. We can make the maximum use of this source for fuelling our automobiles. The *PV cells fitted in Solar panels* can directly convert the Solar Energy into Electric Energy.

This energy can be used to run the car engine. Also, in the absence of sunlight, these solar powered vehicles can store energy and run on the backup.

Some examples of solar powered vehicles are:

Solar Cars – Reva, a solar powered car made by an Indian company can travel upto 8 km in a day.

Solar Ships – The Turanor Planet Solar, a 30m long and 15.2m wide yacht is the world's biggest *solar powered boat*. It has an area of about 470 sq.m. of the solar panel.

Solar Aircraft – A lightweight solar-powered plane named *Qinetiq Zephyr*, flew in the Arizonian sky for over 336 hours. It was developed by the United Kingdom.

Electricity

Electric powered vehicles are of *three types*:

- Directly powered from external power stations
- Powered by stored electricity
- Powered by an on-board electrical generator

These vehicles use direct electricity to generate power in their engines. Major car makers like *Ford Motors, Toyota Motors, Mitsubishi*, etc are developing new generation electric vehicles. *Nissan* has manufactured their 100 percent electric car named the *Nissan Leaf*.

Although many public means of transport across the world like *trams* and *rapid transit systems* use electricity, but the main aim is to bring private transportation under this wing. There are millions of private automobiles running on fuels like petrol and diesel across the world. If even 50 percent of these are replaced by solar powered or electric powered vehicles, the *ecological balance* could be sustained.

Quick Facts

- Non-renewable sources of energy are those substances which cannot be produced in a short period of time. For example, coal, petrol and diesel are non-renewable sources as they take millions of years to form.

- Designed by 21-year-old Yuhan Zhang, the Volkswagen Aqua is an all-terrain hovercraft. It has an imminent approach of futuristic means of transportation powered by hydrogen and driven by impeller. Moreover, it can easily maneuver on lakes, rivers and coastal waters, to the roads, wetlands and snow and ice, with four little electric motorized fans that provide lift and thrust along with a hydrogen cell powered engine.

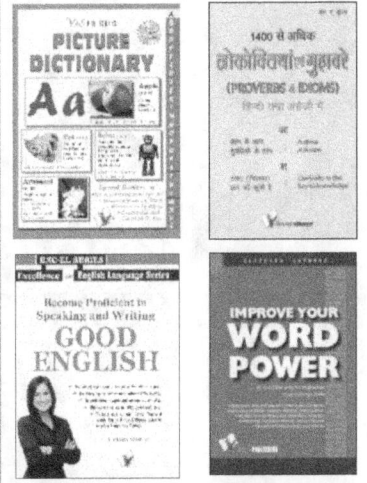

STUDENT DEVELOPMENT/LEARNING

POPULAR SCIENCE

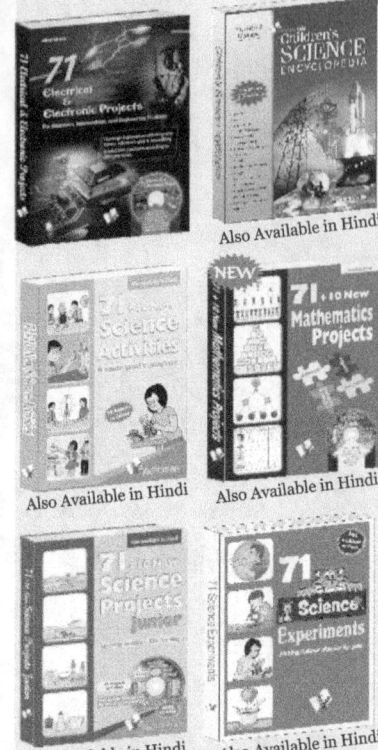

Also Available in Hindi

Also Available in Hindi

Also Available in Hindi

Also Available in Hindi

Also Available in Hindi

Also Available in Hindi

Also Available in Hindi

Also Available in Hindi, Tamil & Bangla

PUZZLES

DRAWING BOOKS

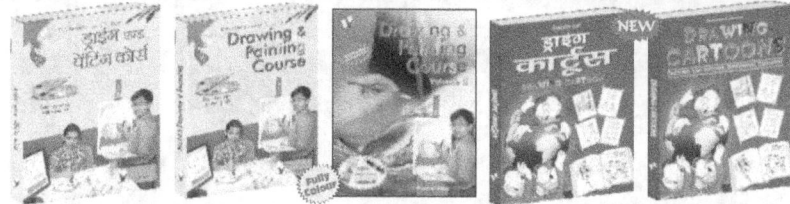

CHILDREN'S ENCYCLOPEDIA – THE WORLD OF KNOWLEDGE

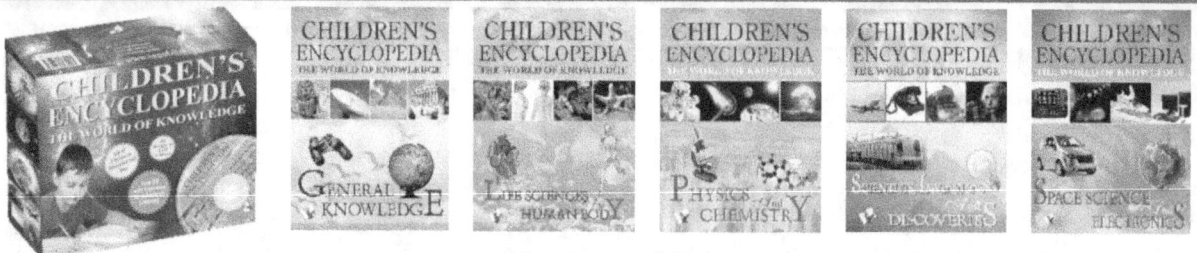

Contact us at sales@vspublishers.com

HINDI LITERATURE

MUSIC/MYSTERIES/MAGIC & FACT

Also Available in Hindi

TALES & STORIES

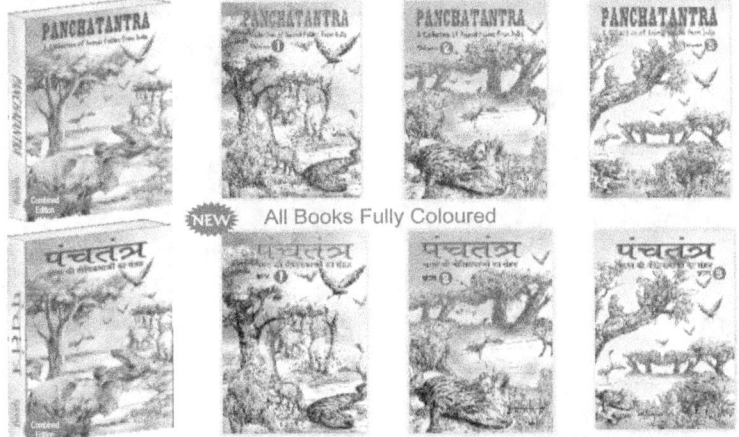

NEW All Books Fully Coloured

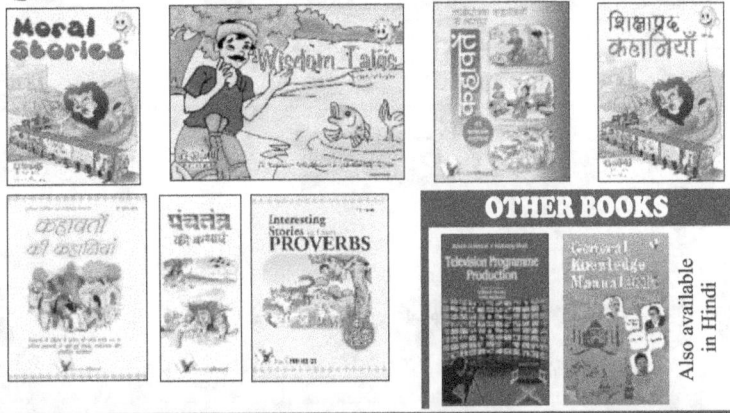

OTHER BOOKS

Also available in Hindi

CHILDREN TALES (बच्चों की कहानियाँ)

www.ingramcontent.com/pod-product-compliance
Lightning Source LLC
LaVergne TN
LVHW080358090426
835513LV00038B/1233

9 789350 579183